MIGHTY MACHINES

Big Rigs

by Kay Manolis

BELLWETHER MEDIA · MINNEAPOLIS, MN

BLASTOFF! READERS

Note to Librarians, Teachers, and Parents:

Blastoff! Readers are carefully developed by literacy experts and combine standards-based content with developmentally appropriate text.

Level 1 provides the most support through repetition of high-frequency words, light text, predictable sentence patterns, and strong visual support.

Level 2 offers early readers a bit more challenge through varied simple sentences, increased text load, and less repetition of high-frequency words.

Level 3 advances early-fluent readers toward fluency through increased text and concept load, less reliance on visuals, longer sentences, and more literary language.

Level 4 builds reading stamina by providing more text per page, increased use of punctuation, greater variation in sentence patterns, and increasingly challenging vocabulary.

Level 5 encourages children to move from "learning to read" to "reading to learn" by providing even more text, varied writing styles, and less familiar topics.

Whichever book is right for your reader, Blastoff! Readers are the perfect books to build confidence and encourage a love of reading that will last a lifetime!

This edition first published in 2008 by Bellwether Media.

Library of Congress Cataloging-in-Publication Data
Manolis, Kay.
  Big rigs / by Kay Manolis.
    p. cm. – (Blastoff! readers. Mighty machines)
Summary: "Simple text and full color photographs introduce young readers to big rigs. Intended for students in kindergarten through third grade"–Provided by publisher.
  Includes bibliographical references and index.
  ISBN-13: 978-1-60014-177-5 (hardcover : alk. paper)
  ISBN-10: 1-60014-177-3 (hardcover : alk. paper)
  1. Tractor trailer combinations–Juvenile literature. 2. Trucking–Juvenile literature. I. Title.

TL230.15.M3589 2008
629.224–dc22   2007040368

Contents

Big rigs rumble
down the road.
Big rigs are
very big trucks.

A big rig has
a **tractor**.

tractor

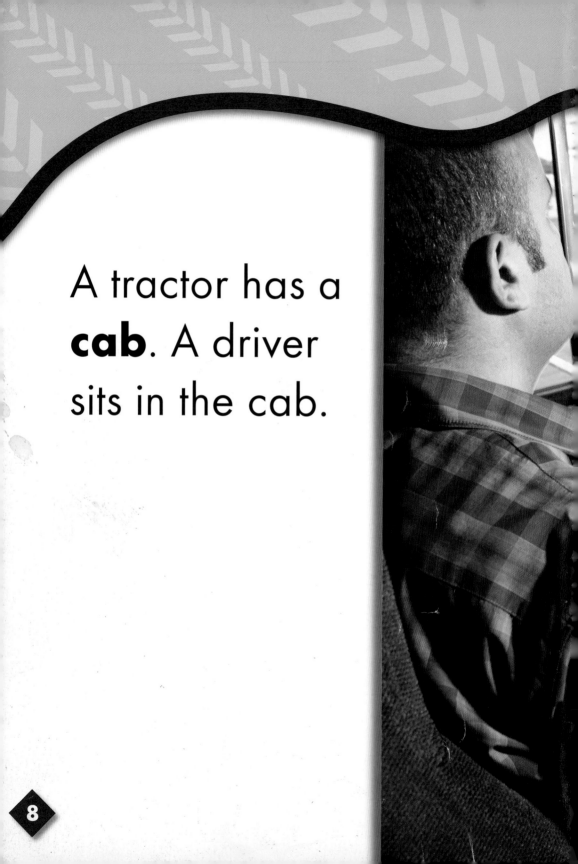

A tractor has a **cab**. A driver sits in the cab.

A tractor has a big **engine**. The engine powers the big rig.

engine

A tractor pulls a **trailer**. A trailer holds **cargo**.

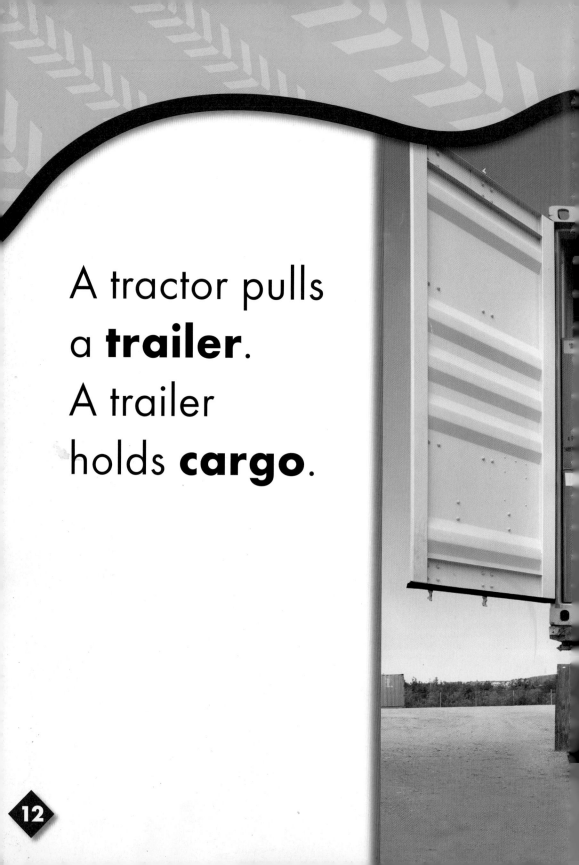

cargo

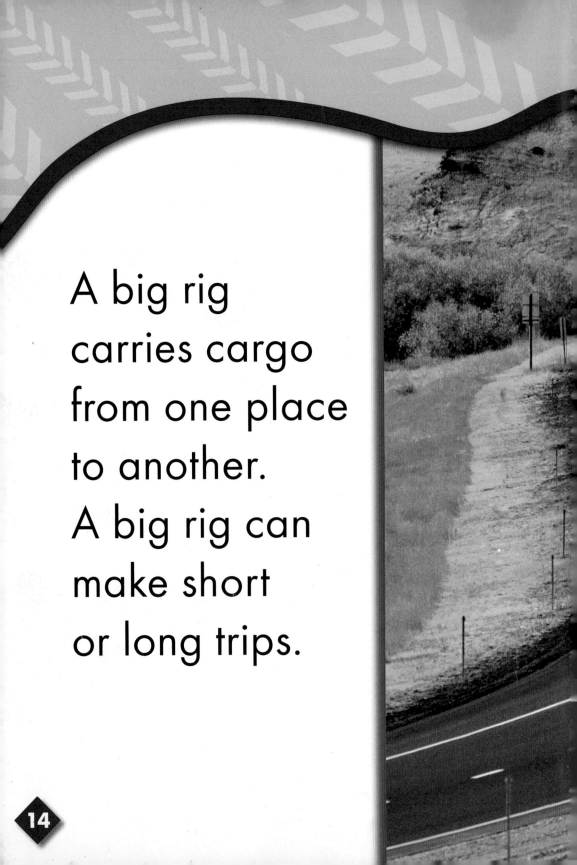

A big rig
carries cargo
from one place
to another.
A big rig can
make short
or long trips.

This big rig
works in
the forest.
It carries logs.

This big rig
is a tanker.
It carries
gasoline.

This big rig
brings carnival
rides to
your town.
Have fun!

FENCE   LIGHTS   SIGNS

Glossary

cab—the part of a tractor where the driver sits

cargo—goods carried by a truck, ship, train, or plane

engine—a machine that makes a vehicle move

gasoline—a type of liquid fuel that powers an engine

tractor—the front part of a big rig

trailer—a piece of equipment that carries cargo and is pulled by a vehicle

To Learn More

AT THE LIBRARY

Mitchell, Joyce Slayton. *Tractor-Trailer Trucker: A Powerful Truck Book*. Berkeley, Calif.: Tricycle Press, 2000.

Molzahn, Arlene Bourgeois. *Trucks and Big Rigs*. Berkeley Heights, N.J.: Enslow, 2003.

Robbins, Ken. *Trucks: Giants of the Highway*. New York: Aladdin, 2002.

Simon, Seymour. *Seymour Simon's Book of Trucks*. New York: HarperCollins, 2000.

ON THE WEB

Learning more about mighty machines is as easy as 1, 2, 3.

1. Go to www.factsurfer.com

2. Enter "mighty machines" into search box.

3. Click the "Surf" button and you will see a list of related web sites.

With factsurfer.com, finding more information is just a click away.

Index

The images in this book are reproduced through the courtesy of: Nancy Brammer, front cover; Roy Ooms/Masterfile, p. 5; Michael Mahovlich/Masterfile, Inc./Alamy, p. 7; Andre Jenny/Alamy, p. 9; Mitch Kezar/Getty Images, p. 11; Lester Lefkowitz/Getty Images, p. 13; Laurance B. Aiuppy/Getty Images, p. 15; Francisco Romero, p. 17; Douglas E. Walker/Masterfile, p. 19; Neil Webster, p. 21.